Public Administratio

Nii Tackie

Public Administration and Policy Making in Ghana

An Introductory Perspective

LAP LAMBERT Academic Publishing

Impressum / Imprint

Bibliografische Information der Deutschen Nationalbibliothek: Die Deutsche Nationalbibliothek verzeichnet diese Publikation in der Deutschen Nationalbibliografie; detaillierte bibliografische Daten sind im Internet über http://dnb.d-nb.de abrufbar.

Alle in diesem Buch genannten Marken und Produktnamen unterliegen warenzeichen-, marken- oder patentrechtlichem Schutz bzw. sind Warenzeichen oder eingetragene Warenzeichen der jeweiligen Inhaber. Die Wiedergabe von Marken, Produktnamen, Gebrauchsnamen, Handelsnamen, Warenbezeichnungen u.s.w. in diesem Werk berechtigt auch ohne besondere Kennzeichnung nicht zu der Annahme, dass solche Namen im Sinne der Warenzeichen- und Markenschutzgesetzgebung als frei zu betrachten wären und daher von jedermann benutzt werden dürften.

Bibliographic information published by the Deutsche Nationalbibliothek: The Deutsche Nationalbibliothek lists this publication in the Deutsche Nationalbibliografie; detailed bibliographic data are available in the Internet at http://dnb.d-nb.de.

Any brand names and product names mentioned in this book are subject to trademark, brand or patent protection and are trademarks or registered trademarks of their respective holders. The use of brand names, product names, common names, trade names, product descriptions etc. even without a particular marking in this works is in no way to be construed to mean that such names may be regarded as unrestricted in respect of trademark and brand protection legislation and could thus be used by anyone.

Coverbild / Cover image: www.ingimage.com

Verlag / Publisher:
LAP LAMBERT Academic Publishing
ist ein Imprint der / is a trademark of
OmniScriptum GmbH & Co. KG
Heinrich-Böcking-Str. 6-8, 66121 Saarbrücken, Deutschland / Germany
Email: info@lap-publishing.com

Herstellung: siehe letzte Seite /
Printed at: see last page
ISBN: 978-3-8383-6097-3

Table of Contents

Chapter 1

Introduction: Defining Public Administration

Milakovich and Gordon define public administration as "all processes, organizations, and individuals acting in official positions associated with carrying out laws and other rules adopted or issued by legislatures, executives, and courts."[1] This means that most of public administration takes place on the executive side especially by the bureaucracy. The bureaucracy, according to Milakovich and Gordon, is "a formal organizational arrangement characterized by division of labor, job specialization with no functional overlap, exercise of authority through a vertical hierarchy, and a system of internal rules, regulations, and record keeping." This definition for public administration will be used as a guide in this book to discuss public administration in Ghana. Milakovich and Gordon also provide a schematic for the government of the U.S. zeroing in on the executive branch based on its role in public administration. This book will also use this schematic as a reference and apply it to Ghana. In other words, the book will develop a schematic for the Government of Ghana by following the style of the afore-mentioned authors.

Although public administration takes place mostly in the executive branch by the definition used in this book, some administration takes place in the legislative and judicial branches too. Therefore, mention is made of these branches and how they impinge on administration. Furthermore, public policy making is closely knit to public administration and, consequently, it is mentioned later in the book from the perspective of the policy process and the structure of the administrative arm of the legislature, the Parliamentary Service. The rest of the book is in five chapters: the principal structures of the executive branch, which focuses on the ministries, public boards, commissions, corporations, and services; the civil service: genesis,

3

key moments, reforms and perspectives, which focuses on the establishment of the civil service, unique history, and highlights; the judiciary and its role, which emphasizes basic structure and pertinent issues of the judiciary; the dynamics of policy making, which covers the policy process and the administration of the legislature; and conclusion: tying all together, which knits all other chapters and thoughts together.

Chapter 2

The Principal Structures of the Executive Branch

The Constitution and Public Administration

Public administration in Ghana emanates from the Constitution of 1992.[2] It clearly states on page 10, Article 11, Clause 1, "The Laws of Ghana shall comprise: (a) this Constitution; (b) enactments made by or under the authority of Parliament established by this Constitution; (c) any Orders, Rules and Regulations made by any person or authority under a power conferred by this Constitution; (d) the existing law; and (e) the common law." In addition, on page 51, Article 58, Clauses 1-3, it states, "(1) The executive authority of Ghana shall vest in the President and shall be exercised in accordance with the provisions of this Constitution. (2) The executive authority of Ghana shall extend to the execution and maintenance of this Constitution and all laws made under or continued in force by this Constitution. (3) Subject to the provisions of this Constitution, the functions conferred on the President by clause (1) of this article may be exercised by him either directly or through officers subordinate to him."

The Ministries

These are the most visible national executive units or organizations. They are led by ministers who are also members of the cabinet. There are 24 ministries in the national executive branch;[3] these have been mentioned or grouped here according to the divisions or nomenclature given by Adum-Yeboah[4], namely, Ministry of Finance, Ministry of Food and Agriculture, Ministry of Fisheries and Aquaculture Development, Ministry of Lands and Natural Resources, Ministry of Trade and Industry, Ministry of Tourism, Culture and Creative Arts, Ministry of Energy and Petroleum, and Ministry of Environment, Science, Technology and Innovation (Economic Sector); Ministry of Water Resources, Works and Housing, Ministry of

Transport, Ministry of Roads and Highways, and Ministry of Communications (Infrastructure Sector); Ministry of Education, Ministry of Youth and Sports, Ministry of Employment and Labor Relations, Ministry of Health, and Ministry of Gender, Children and Social Protection (Social Sector); Ministry of Local Government and Rural Development, Ministry of Foreign Affairs and Regional Integration, Ministry of Information and Media Relations, and Ministry of Chieftaincy and Traditional Affairs (Administration Sector); Ministry of Justice and Attorney General's Department, Ministry of Defense, and Ministry of Interior (Public Safety Sector) (See Figure 1, Appendix).

The ministries have departments or divisions within them, and are also affiliated with or directly oversee other agencies. At this juncture, six examples of ministries with their associated divisions and/or agencies are provided. The first is the Ministry of Finance. The main divisions of the Ministry are Budget, Debt Management, Economic Research and Forecasting, External Economic Relations, Financial Sector, General Administration, Information and Communication Technology, Internal Audit, Legal, Public Investment, and Real Sector. Agencies overseen by the Ministry are the Controller and Accountant General's Department, Securities and Exchange Commission, Institute of Accounting Training, Ghana Revenue Authority, Bank of Ghana, National Lotteries Authority, Public Procurement Authority, and Ghana Cocoa Board.[5] The second is the Ministry of Food and Agriculture. There are two main sets of divisions, called directorates, in this Ministry, and within each main directorate are the individual or sub directorates. They are Finance and Administration; Human Resource Development and Management; Policy, Planning, Monitoring, and Evaluation; Statistics Research and Information (Line Directorates); Agricultural Engineering Services; Agricultural Extension Services; Animal Production; Crop Services; Fisheries;

6

Plant Protection and Regulatory Services; Veterinary Services; and Women in Agricultural Development (Technical Directorates). Agencies overseen by or affiliated with the Ministry are the Irrigation Development Authority; Irrigation Company of Upper Region; and National Buffer Stock Company.[6] The third is the Ministry of Transport. The divisions within the Ministry are Monitoring and Evaluation, Policy and Planning, Research Statistics and Information Management, and Finance and Administration. Agencies under the Ministry are Ghana Airport Company Limited, Ghana Civil Aviation Authority, Driver and Vehicle Licensing Authority, National Road Safety Commission, Metro Mass Transit Limited, Government Technical Training Center, Ghana Ports and Harbors Authority, Regional Maritime University, Volta Lake Transport Company, Ghana Railway Company Limited, and Ghana Railway Development Authority.[7] The fourth is the Ministry of Health. Divisions here include Policy, Planning, Monitoring and Evaluation; Human Resource for Health Development; Research Statistics and Information Management; Procurement and Supply; Traditional and Alternative Medicines; Finance; General Administration; and Internal Audit. A key agency affiliated with the Ministry is the Ghana Health Service.[8] The fifth is the Ministry of Information and Media Relations. The key divisions here are General Administration, and Information Services Department. Agencies affiliated with or overseen by the Ministry are the Ghana News Agency, Ghana Broadcasting Corporation, and Ghana Film and Television Institute.[9] The sixth and final is the Ministry of Justice and Attorney General's Department. The agencies overseen by the Ministry are the Council for Law Reporting, Legal Aid Board, Law Reform Commission, Serious Frauds Office, Ghana School of Law, and Registrar's General Department.[10]

Public Boards, Commissions, Corporations and Services

Apart from the ministries, all other public entities derive from Article 190 of the 1992 Constitution. For instance, Clause 1, page 128, states, "The Public Services of Ghana shall include (a) the Civil Service; the Judicial Service; the Audit Service; the Education Service; the Prisons Service; the Parliamentary Service; the Health Service; the Statistical Service; the National Fire Service; the Customs, Excise and Preventive Service; the Internal Revenue Service; the Police Service; the Immigration Service, and the Legal Service; (b) public corporation other than those set up as commercial ventures; (c) public services established by this Constitution; and (d) such other public services as Parliament may by law prescribe."[11] In addition, respectively, Articles 193, 194, and 196 on pages 129 and 131 elucidate further the role of the public service. Article 193 states, "(1) The President shall, acting in accordance with the advice of the Public Services Commission, appoint a public officer as the Head of the Civil Service. (2) Subject to the provisions of this Constitution, the Head of the Civil Service shall not hold any other public office." Article 194 states, "(1) There shall be a Public Services Commission which shall perform such functions as assigned to it by this Constitution or by any other law." Article 196 further indicates, "the Public Services Commission shall have such powers and exercise such supervisory, regulatory and consultative functions as Parliament shall, by law, prescribe, including as may be applicable, the supervision and regulation of entrance and promotion examinations, recruitment and appointment into or promotions within, the public services, and the establishment of standards and guidelines on the terms and conditions of employment in the public services."

From the above, it can be seen that the Public Services Commission and Office of the Head of Civil Service (OHCS) are key agencies in the public service.

As a result of this, the two agencies are given further discussion. The Public Services Commission Act, 1994 (or Act 482) gives a detail description of the Commission, its functions, and its supporting Secretariat. The functions of the Commission are: (1) to advise Government on the criteria for appointment to public offices as well as persons to hold or act in public offices; (2) to promote efficiency, accountability and integrity in the Public Services; (3) to prescribe appropriate systems and procedures for the management of personnel records within the Public Services; (4) to identify, explore and promote the recruitment of suitable personnel into the Public Services, acting in collaboration with educational institutions; (5) to undertake planning of the manpower requirements of the Public Services, using data from the educational institutions and other sources; (6) To improve recruitment policies and techniques by introducing modern methods of judging the suitability of officers; (7) to conduct examinations and interviews for appointments to posts, and for promotions in the Public Services or within Public Corporations to ensure uniformity of standards of selection and qualification; (8) to provide a standard framework for evaluating and classifying jobs in the Public Services; (9) to review the organization, structure and manpower requirements of agencies and bodies in the Public Services and advise Government on such manpower rationalization as may be necessary for maximum utilization of human resources in the Public Services; (10) to oversee the human resource development activities of Public Services organizations to ensure career planning and career development in the Public Services; (11) to conduct, in collaboration with training institutions, personnel research into human resources management in the Public Services in order to improve personnel practices and their utilization in the Public Services; and (12) to perform any other duties assigned to it under the Constitution or any other enactment.[12]

The Civil Service is the largest employer in Ghana, and it is the hub of the bureaucracy. According to Kiggundu, "the Civil Service comprises all those employees working for the national government, employed by the authority of the Public Services Commission, and paid directly through the government payroll."[13] The current Civil Service was created by the Civil Service Law, PNDCL 327, 1993. Section 4 of the Law identifies who is a member of the Civil Service: "(a) A person serving in a civil capacity in a post designated as a Ghana Civil Service post by or under the Law in: (1) The Office of the President; (2) A Ministry; (3) A government department/agency at the national, regional, and district levels; (4) Any other Civil Service department established under the authority of the Law the emoluments attached to which are paid directly from the Consolidated Fund or any other source approved by the government; (b) A person holding a post designated as a Civil Service post created by or under the authority of any other enactment, the emoluments attached to which are paid directly from the Consolidated Fund or any other source approved by the government.[14] The Law also created the OHCS. The Law states, among other things, that "the Civil Service forms part of the Public Services of Ghana, and that it comprises service in a civil office of Government." The OHCS's mission is to "promote and ensure continuous renewal and professional development of the Human Resource of the Civil Service by ensuring that the Ministries, Departments and Agencies are optimally structured, adequately staffed with the right skills mix to provide policy advice to Ghana's political leadership to facilitate good governance and accelerated national development." In order to achieve its mission, PNDCL 327 specifies the following functions for the Service: "(1) initiate and formulate policy options for the government; (2) initiate and advise on government plans; (3) undertake such research as may be necessary for the effective implementation of government principles; (4) implement

10

government policies; (5) review government policies and plans; (6) monitor, coordinate, and evaluate government policies and plans; (7) perform such functions as are incidental or conducive to the achievement of the object specified in this Law; and (8) perform such other functions as the Executive may direct."[15]

The Civil Service of Ghana is overseen by the Civil Service Council, which is the governing body for the entire Civil Service. It gives general policy direction to the Service. Below the Council is the Head of Civil Service, who is the leader of the Ghana Civil Service, a "chief executive officer" so to speak. He or she is responsible for the day-to-day operation of the Civil Service. Immediately subordinate to the Head of Civil Service is the Chief Director, the bureaucratic leader of the Service. The Chief Director is the advisor-in-chief to the Head of Civil Service on all matters regarding the operations of the Office of Head of Civil Service (OHCS) specifically, and the entire Civil Service. In addition, the Chief Director coordinates the activities of the various directorates and units of the OHCS. These directorates and units are the Public Records and Archives Administration Department; Management Services Division; Research Statistical Information Management; Recruitment and Training Directorate; Career Management Directorate; Policy and Standards Directorate; Performance Monitoring, Evaluation Directorate; and Finance and Administration Directorate.[16]

There are several public boards, commissions, corporations, and other agencies in Ghana under the purview of the Public Services Commission and/or the OHSC. However, only seven examples are provided here for illustrative purposes. These are the Social Security and National Insurance Trust (SSNIT), Bank of Ghana, Controller and Accountant General's Department, Ghana Standards Authority, Food and Drugs Authority, Ghana Ports and Harbors Authority, and Lands Commission. Some of these entities have more flexibility to operate than others. For instance, SSNIT is statutory public Trust charged with the administration of the nation's pension scheme. It has the responsibility of replacing part of the lost income due to old age, invalidity, and payment of survivor's benefits to dependants of deceased employees. SSNIT derives its authority from the National Pensions Act of 2008, Act 766, which is based on a three-tier pension scheme. The scheme is self-financing through the contribution of members and return on investments of funds. The rate of contribution is 18.5% of earnings of members; employers contribute 13.0% and employees contribute 5.5%. The key functions of SSNIT are as follows: (1) register employers and employees; (2) collect contributions; (3) manage records on members; (4) invest funds of the Scheme; and (5) process and pay benefits to eligible members and nominated dependants. The activities of SSNIT are decentralized and are carried out in 48 branches and 18 day offices, overseen by seven area offices, and supervised by the Operations Coordinator. In addition, it has an executive committee headed by the Director-General, which oversees the day-to-day operations, and a board of trustees which gives the policy direction of the agency.[17]

The Bank of Ghana operates under the Bank of Ghana Act of 2002, Act 612. The key functions of the Bank are: (1) formulate and implement monetary policy aimed at achieving the objects of the Bank; (2) promote by monetary measure the stabilization of the value of the currency within and outside Ghana; (3) institute measures which are likely to have a favorable effect on the balance of payments, the state of public finances and the general development of the national economy; (4) regulate, supervise and direct the banking and credit system and ensure the smooth operation of the financial sector; (5) promote, regulate and supervise payment and settlement systems; (6) issue and redeem the currency notes and coins; (7) ensure effective maintenance and management of Ghana's external

12

financial services; (8) license, regulate, promote and supervise non-banking financial institutions; (9) act as banker and financial adviser to the Government; (10) promote and maintain relations with international banking and financial institutions and subject to the Constitution or any other relevant enactment, implement international monetary agreements to which Ghana is a party; and (11) do all other things that are identical or conducive to the efficient performance of its functions under this Act and any other enactment. The governing body of the Bank is the Board of Directors, which is headed by the Governor as chairman. Also, the Board comprises two Deputy Governors and nine non-executive directors. The Board is charged with formulating policies needed for the achievement of the Bank's objectives. These objectives are: (1) to maintain stability in the general level of prices; and (2) to ensure effective and efficient operations of banking and credit systems and support general economic growth. For illustrative purposes, the organizational chart of the Bank is shown as Figure 2 in the Appendix. It shows that the Bank operates through several Departments.[18]

The Controller and Accountant General's Department (CAGD) was established under the Civil Service Act of 1960, CA5. Its operation and authority is strengthened by the Financial Administrative Act of 2003, Act 654. The Department is headed by the Controller and Accountant-General (CAG). The CAG is the Government's Chief Accounting Officer, and is the Chief Adviser to the Minister of Finance and the Government on accounting matters. The CAGD is mandated to: (1) receive all Public and Trust monies payable into the Consolidated Fund; (2) provide secure custody of Public and Trust monies (with the support of the Ministry of Finance and Bank of Ghana); (3) make disbursements on behalf of the Government (including the payment of monthly salaries to government employees inactive service; pension gratuity and monthly pension payment to those

13

on retirement; and releases of funds to prosecute government projects and development throughout the country); (4) pay all Government workers' wages, salaries and allowances; (5) process and pay all pension gratuity for the Civil Service; (6) establish, on behalf of government, such accounts with the Bank of Ghana and its agents for the deposit of Public and Trust monies; (7) be solely responsible for the opening of bank accounts for any government department; (8) keep, prepare, render and publish financial statements on the Consolidated Fund of Ghana both monthly and annually (not later than three months after the end of the financial year); (9) approve accounting instructions for Government departments; and (10) promote the development of efficient accounting systems in all Government departments. The Controller and Accountant General's Department operates under six main divisions: Finance and Administration; Treasury; Financial Management Services; Information Communication and Technology; Payroll; and Audit and Investigation.[19]

The Ghana Standards Authority operates under the Standards Decree of 1973, NRCD 173, and Weights and Measures Decree of 1975, NRCD 326. The Authority is mandated to undertake: (1) national standards development and dissemination; (2) testing services; (3) inspection services; (4) product certification scheme; (5) calibration, verification and inspection of weights, measures, and weighing and measuring instruments; (6) pattern approval of new weighing and measuring instruments; (7) destination inspection of imported high risk goods; (8) promoting quality management systems in industry; and (9) advice the Ministry of Trade and Industry, on Standards and related issues. The Authority operates through seven divisions and various departments. The seven divisions are Standards, Metrology, Finance, Administration, Testing, Certification, and

14

Inspectorate. The organizational chart is shown as Figure 3 in the Appendix. It shows a very elaborative organizational or operational structure.[20]

The Food and Drugs Authority was established under the Public Health Act 2012, Act 851. This Act supersedes the Food and Drugs Act of 1992, PNDCL 305B. The law gave the Authority the mandate to provide and enforce standards for the sale of food, herbal medicinal products, cosmetics, drugs, medical devices and household chemical substances. The functions of the Authority are as follows: (1) ensure adequate and effective standards for food, drugs, cosmetics, household chemicals and medical devices; (2) monitor through the District Assemblies and any other agency of State compliance with the provisions of this Part [of the Act]; (3) advise the Minister on measures for the protection of the health of consumers; (4) advise the Minister on the preparation of effective regulations for the implementation of this Part [of the Act]; (5) approve the initiation and conduct of clinical trials in the country; and (6) perform any other functions that are ancillary to attaining the objects of the Authority. The Authority is governed by a board; however, management, led by a chief executive officer, is responsible for the day-to-day operation of the organization. The Food and Drugs Authority carries out its operations through two key divisions; the divisions are divided into departments. Also, there are other departments and operational units within the Authority. The two divisions are the Food Division and the Drugs Division. The other departments and operational units are the Regional Offices; Administration Department; Finance Department; Audit Department; Human Resource Unit; Import and Export Control Department; Project, Research and Management Information System Department; Laboratory Service Department; Internal Audit Unit; and Public Communications and Education Unit.[21]

15

The Ghana Ports and Harbors Authority is a statutory corporation that operates based on the Provisional National Defence Council Law of 1986, PNDCL 160. It is tasked with the responsibility of planning, building, managing, maintaining, and operating the seaports of Ghana. The Authority has the following functions: (1) provide in a port such facilities as appear to be necessary for the efficient and proper operation of the port; (2) maintain the port facilities, extend and enlarge any such facilities as it shall deem fit; (3) regulate the use of any port and of the port facilities; (4) maintain and deepen as necessary the approaches to, and the navigable waters within and outside the limits of any port, and also maintain lightness and beacons and other navigational service and aids as appear to it to be necessary; (5) provide facilities for the transport, storage, warehousing, loading, unloading and sorting of goods passing through any port, and operate road haulage services for hire or reward; (6) carry on all the business of stevedoring, master porterage and lighterage services; and (7) generally discharge any other functions which are necessary or incidental to the foregoing. The Ghana Ports and Harbors Authority also carries out its operations through several divisions and departments, such as Operations, Corporate Planning, Public Affairs, Administration, Legal and Insurance, and Audit.[22]

The Lands Commission was established under the Lands Commission Act of 2008, Act 767. The objectives of the Commission are to: (1) promote the judicious use of land by the society and ensure that land use is in accordance with sustainable management principles and maintenance of sound ecosystem; and (2) ensure that land development is effected in conformity with the nation's development goals. Furthermore, the functions of the Commission are as follows: (1) on behalf of the Government, manage public lands and any other lands vested in the President by the Constitution or by any other law and any lands vested in the Commission; (2)

advise the Government, local authorities and traditional authorities on the policy framework for the development of particular areas of the country to ensure that the development of individual pieces of land is coordinated with the relevant development plan for the area concerned; (3) formulate and submit to Government recommendations on national policy with respect to land use suitability or capability; (4) advise on, and assist in the execution of, a comprehensive program for the registration of title to land as well as registration of deeds and instruments affecting land throughout the country; (5) facilitate the acquisition of land on behalf of [the] Government; (6) establish standards for and regulate survey and mapping of the country and provide survey and mapping services where necessary; (7) license practitioners of cadastral surveys; (8) undertake land and land related valuation services; (9) ensure that socioeconomic activities are consistent with sound land use through sustainable land use planning in the long-term national interest; (10) instill order and discipline into the land market through curbing the incidence of land encroachment, unapproved development schemes, multiple or illegal land sales, land speculation and other forms of land racketeering; (11) minimize or eliminate, where possible, the sources of protracted land boundary disputes, conflicts and litigations in order to bring their associated economic costs and sociopolitical upheavals under control; (12) promote community participation and public awareness at all levels in sustainable land management practices to ensure the highest and best use of land; (13) promote research into all aspects of land ownership, tenure and the operations of land market, and land development process; (14) improve and collect levies, fees, charges for services rendered; (15) establish and maintain a comprehensive land information system; and (16) perform other functions the Ministry [of Lands and Natural Resources] may assign to it. Moreover, the Commission has to collaborate and coordinate with the following

17

institutions in the performance of its functions: (1) Office of the Administration of Stool Lands; (2) Town and Country Planning Department; (3) Structures designed for the customary administration of stool, skin, family or community-owned land, or any other land; and (4) other public agencies, government bodies and any other private body that has operations or activities relevant to the functions of the Commission. As other entities described before, the Lands Commission carries out its operations through four divisions and several departments. The divisions are the Survey and Mapping, Land Registration, Land Valuation, and Public and Vested Lands Management.[23]

Specialized Independent Commissions

Apart from the regular public commissions, there are also specialized independent commissions that play critical roles in day-to-day public administration. Two such commissions are the Commission on Human Rights and Administrative Justice (CHRAJ) and the National Commission for Civic Education (NCCE). The CHRAJ obtains its power from the 1992 Constitution and was established under the Commission on Human Rights and Administrative Justice Act of 1993, Act 456. Its role is to protect and promote fundamental rights and freedoms and administrative justice. The functions of the Commission are to: (1) investigate complaints of violations of fundamental rights and freedoms, injustice, corruption, abuse of power and unfair treatment of any person by a public officer in the exercise of his official duties; (2) investigate complaints concerning the functioning of the Public Services Commission, the administrative organs of the State, the offices of the Regional Coordinating Council and the District Assembly, the Armed Forces, the Police Service and the Prison Service insofar as the complaints relate to the failure to achieve a balanced structuring of those services or equal access by all to the recruitment of those services or fair administration in

18

relation to those services; (3) investigate complaints concerning practices and actions by persons, private enterprises and other institutions where those complaints allege violations of fundamental rights and freedoms under the Constitution; (4) take appropriate action to call for the remedying, correction and reversal of instances specified in paragraphs (1), (2), and (3) through such means as are fair, proper and effective, including (a) negotiation and compromise between parties concerned; (b) causing the complaint and its finding on it to be reported to the superior of the offending person; (c) bringing proceedings in a competent court for a remedy to secure the termination of the offending action or conduct, or the abandonment or alteration of the offending procedures; and (d) bringing proceedings to restrain the enforcement of such legislation or regulation by challenging its validity if the offending action or conduct is sought to be justified by subordinate legislation or regulation which is unreasonable or otherwise ultra vires; (5) investigate allegations that a public officer has contravened or has not complied with a provision of Chapter Twenty-four (Code of Conduct for Public Officers) of the Constitution; (6) investigate all instances of alleged or suspected corruption and the misappropriation of public monies by officials and to take appropriate steps, including reports to the Attorney-General and Auditor-General, resulting from such investigation; (7) educate the public as to human rights and freedoms by such means as the Commissioner may decide, including publications, lectures and symposia; and (8) report annually to Parliament on the performance of its functions.[24]

In addition, the Commission has the power to: (1) issue subpoenas requiring the attendance of any person before the Commission and the production of any document or record relevant to any investigation by the Commission; (2) cause any person contemptuous of any such subpoena to be prosecuted before a competent court; (3) question any person in respect of any subject matter under investigation before the Commission; (4) require any person to disclose truthfully and frankly any information within his knowledge relevant to any investigation by the Commissioner. On the contrary, the Commission shall not investigate: (1) a matter which is pending before a court or judicial tribunal; or (2) a matter involving the relations or dealings between Government and any other Government or an international organization; or (3) a matter relating to the exercise of the prerogative of mercy. The CHRAJ is headed by a chair and two deputy chairs; its operations are conducted through four departments, namely, Legal Investigations Department, Anti-Corruption Department, Public Education Department, and Finance and Administration Department. The Commission also has ten regional offices .[25]

The NCCE also derives its power from the 1992 Constitution, and was established in 1993 by Act 452. The NCCE is mandated to promote the 1992 Constitution as a whole and also create awareness among the populace of their rights and responsibilities. The functions of the NCCE in Article 233 of the Constitution, pages 148-149, are: "(a) to create and sustain within the society the awareness of the principles and objectives of this Constitution as the fundamental law of the people of Ghana; (b) to educate and encourage the public to defend this Constitution at all times, against all forms of abuse and violation; (c) to formulate for the consideration of Government, from time to time, programs at the national, regional and district levels aimed at realizing the objectives of this Constitution; (d) to formulate, implement and oversee programs intended to inculcate in the citizens of Ghana awareness of their civic responsibilities and an appreciation of their rights and obligations as free people; and (e) such other functions as Parliament may prescribe." Based on its mandate and functions, the NCCE develops and implements different programs and projects. Of particular importance, is "Project

Citizen," which encourages youth participation in democracy. It equips students to participate effectively in solving problems in their communities. The operation of the NCCE is carried out by a chairman, two deputy chairmen, and four others. A critical department in the NCCE is the Research, Gender and Equality Department, which is led by a director and two deputy directors. Other officers include senior civic education officers, civic education officers, assistant civic education officers and field officers. The main function of the department is to conduct research on socioeconomic and political issues related to the Constitution.[26]

Chapter 3

The Civil Service: Genesis, Key Moments, Reforms, and Perspectives

The Civil Service has its roots in the Colonial Service of the Gold Coast, under British rule. Its genesis can be traced back to 1843. The functions were: (1) maintenance of law and order; (2) imposition and collection of taxes; and (3) exploitation of the rich mineral deposits and other natural resources of the Colony. The Head of the Civil Service then was the Governor, and next after him was the Colonial Secretary, who run the day-to-day affairs of the Service from the Secretariat. Next to the Colonial Secretary were the Financial Secretary, the Attorney General, and the Auditor General. Below the Secretariat were the various departments, their heads, and personnel.[27]

Between 1925 and 1926, Sir Gordon Guggisburg, the Governor, decided to implement an Africanization of Civil Service Plan, which included increasing the number of locals holding appointments; decreasing the high cost of hiring Europeans; and creating a local formula for accelerated development. Furthermore, several initiatives were taken as a result of the Lynch Commission Report, 1941. The initiatives included a scholarship program to ensure training for personnel, 1941; formation of an interim Public Services Commission, 1948; development of a process for educating and training locals to take up senior positions in the Civil Service. As a result of the Libury Commission Report 1951, genuine efforts were made to reform the structures of the government and the public service. Among the recommendations of the Commission were (1) redesigning of the structure of the machinery of government; (2) restructuring of the Civil Service; (3) establishment of statutory corporations to assume certain functions of government; and (4) new salary structure and conditions of service. The restructuring of the Civil Service was based on the British System, and therefore, Departments and portfolios in the

22

Colonial Civil Service were converted to Ministries in 1951 when the Gold Coast gained internal self-rule. Since that time, many Ministries and/or Departments have been created, restructured, or realigned depending on the need.[28]

In 1957, when Ghana gained independence, civil servants became the main channels through which the government implemented its agenda of development and public welfare. In addition, in 1960, the National Assembly passed the Civil Service Act of 1960 (CA5). Among other things, it made provision for the following: (1) the creation of Civil Service posts; (2) setting up of Ministries and Departments; (3) appointment and retirement of civil servants; and (4) conditions of service, disciplinary proceedings and other matters relating to the Civil Service. This Act was later complemented by the Civil Service (Interim) Regulations of 1960 (LI 47); the regulations included, but not limited to, the following: (1) the creation of a Ghana Civil Service Commission; (2) the structure of the Ghana Civil Service; and (3) the filling of vacancies in the Ghana Civil Service. In September 1965, the National Assembly passed the Civil Service (Amendment) Act of 1965 (Act 303). A key feature of this Act was the creation of the Establishment Secretariat and the creation of Head of Civil Service and Secretary to the Cabinet. These laws (Civil Service Act, 1960; Civil Service Interim Regulations, 1960; and Civil Service [Amendment] Act, 1965) were the main laws of the land until the promulgation of the 1992 Constitution, and the subsequent passage of the Civil Service Law, PNDCL 327, of 1993. The latter law made the Civil Service part of the Public Services, and indicated it comprised both central and local governments. Later on, Local Government Act 462 and Local Government Service Act 656 were passed to govern the operations of the local government system.[29]

The characteristics of an efficient Civil Service are indicated by Agyekum-Dwamena as: (1) high levels of professional/technical performance in terms of efficiency, effectiveness and initiative, with well-trained staff who are knowledgeable, proactive, and responsive to the aspirations of the government and the people; (2) integrity, fairness, impartiality and incorruptibility; (3) high motivation and commitment; (4) discipline, accountability, and transparency; and (4) political impartiality.[30] However, in previous years, especially in the late 1970s and 1980s, these characteristics were lacking in the Ghanaian Civil Service due to degeneration. Adei and Boachie-Danquah provide external reasons for the degeneration and the reasons include: (1) political instability; (2) bad governance; (3) economic decline; and (4) the politicization of the Civil Service. Additionally, internal reasons include: (1) the scarcity of financial, material, and equipment resources; (2) human resource capacity: associated with this, were skills shortage in critical areas such as policy analysis, financial management and procurement; (3) low morale and motivation linked to a decline in discipline and work ethic, which in turn led to low productivity and performance; and (4) a lack of customer orientation.[31]

Similarly, Agyekum-Dwamena describes the characteristics of the Ghanaian Civil Service as one plagued by: (1) lack of vision and clear sense of direction; (2) inappropriate structures and systems; (3) ineffective leadership and weak management; (4) low morale and negative corporate image; (5) excessive bureaucratic delays; (6) low capacity for planning and implementation of policy programs and projects; (7) lack of discipline; (8) shortage of skilled manpower; (9) corruption; (10) poor working environment, inadequate tools and offices often in a sordid state of disrepair; and (11) low remuneration and poor conditions of service.[32] Kiggundu also mentions commonly cited causes of Civil Service ineffectiveness in Ghana as: (1) poor morale; (2) poor pay, benefits and incentives; (3) high levels of absenteeism; (4) inadequate supervision; (5) ineffective promotion and career development policies and procedures; (6) poor performance appraisal practices; (7) poorly designed jobs; poor human resource management; and (8) hostile environment.[33]

As a result of these weaknesses in the Civil Service, several reform initiatives such as the Civil Service Reform Program (CSRP) and the Civil Service Performance Improvement Program (CSPIP) were implemented. The CSRP, 1987-1993, was put in place to reduce the constraints that prevented the Civil Service from functioning as an agent of change. It was part of the Structural Adjustment Program (SAP), which was in vogue at the time. The SAP was a type of austerity accompanied by institutional restructuring. The broad objective of the CSRP was to "restructure the Civil Service in such a way as to make it more productive, effective and efficient, and strengthen its capacity for the implementation of development programs." Specific objectives were: "control of the size of the Civil Service; improve pay and grading; reform of organization and management; planning and strengthening of training; and management of retrenchment and redeployment." Although there were some achievements for the CSRP, such as the introduction of new performance appraisal system; using merit rather than longevity for promotion; and revision of the Civil Service Law, the impact of the CSRP was unimpressive. The main objective of making the Civil Service effective and efficient was not achieved because of some challenges such as: it was a top-down program and the rank and file of the Civil Service did not feel part of it; there was over-emphasis on the Office of Head of Civil Service and not on the ministries, other departments, and agencies; lack of adequate capacity to monitor prior actions; ad-hoc nature of oversight and reforms; and incongruence between donor deadlines and government implementation schedules.[34]

Based on the foregoing, the CSPIP was introduced in 1995. The CSPIP was part of the National Institutional Renewal Program (NIRP), which solely focused on the Civil Service. The broad objectives of the CSPIP were to: (1) rectify the shortcomings and the critical implementation gaps identified in the CSRP; (2) promote and enhance Civil Service performance, service delivery systems and good governance with particular emphasis on transparency and accountability; and (3) achieve and sustain growth rates from 5% to between 8-10% in the medium-term. Indeed, the implication was the CSPIP was to improve the capacity of the Civil Service and all its associated institutions to become one with a higher level of efficiency. In order to achieve and maintain effective capacity building, individual institutions were asked to take responsibility for their capacity diagnosis and development activities. The underpinning tenets of this approach were participation, consensus building, enhancing commitment, and creating a sense of ownership. To be fair, CSPIP had some success, such as formation of capacity development teams; administration of self-appraisal instruments; conducting beneficial surveys; conducting diagnostic workshops; and producing of performance improvement plans. These modest achievements notwithstanding, the Civil Service at the end of the first phase of CSPIP had problems that included relatively poor remuneration, and low morale and lack of basic logistics. Professionalization of the Civil Service, and tackling inadequate salary and incentives were suggested as implementation items for the second phase of CSPIP.[35]

Ayee, Adei and Boachie-Danquah, and Agyekum-Dwamena recommend strategies for a way forward for building a new or effective Civil Service. Ayee indicates that for Civil Service reform to succeed: (1) there must be broad-based ownership and support of the reforms by the political and administrative leadership as well as the rank and file of the Civil Service; (2) before designing programs, there must be an open process of assessing the current situation and then clearly defining a strategy to ameliorate or improve the situation; (3) there must be a meritocratic system in place; (4) there must be a long-term plan in place as reforms cannot be done overnight.[36] Adei and Boachie-Danquah intimate that creative and business-like leadership is needed for Civil Service reforms to succeed rather than creating new instruments for reforms.[37] Agyekum-Dwamena suggests that for Civil Service reforms to succeed, the following are needed: (1) the Service needs leaders who see themselves as change agents who will facilitate requisite reforms; (2) the focus of training programs should be on better service delivery derived from a new human resource management system; (3) there is a need for a new Civil Service regulatory framework that enhances the performance effectiveness and government capacity to deal adequately with the private sector and other society stakeholders; (4) there is a need for modernized procedural system and rules that improve efficiency of service delivery, such as system-wide use of computers and other information technology; (5) there is a need to regenerate integrity in the Civil Service such as enforcing code of conduct and better systems of accountability; and (6) the revision of the salary policy of the Service.[38] Due to the partial successes of previous reforms, the Government of the NDC in 2011 introduced a new reform program, the New Approach to Public Sector Reform (NAPSR). The NAPSR is supposed to be more sector-driven and gives primary responsibility for reforms to sector Ministries. In other words, the Cabinet will see to the day-to-day progress of the NAPSR; the liaising entity for this Reform is the Public Sector Reform Secretariat (PSRS). The PSRS is supposed to advice and identify resources needed by sector Ministers to ensure reform occurs smoothly. Several donors have expressed support for the NAPSR program.[39]

Gymah-Boadi also discusses a developmental public service, of which the Civil Service is a component. A developmental public service means the ability of the public service to help the state to implement and accomplish its goals. It encompasses certain state capacities, namely, regulatory; administrative; technical; and extractive. However, Ghana's Public Service in the past, especially in the 1970s and 1980s, lacked adequate capacity to do these things very well. In short, the task of creating a developmental public service in Ghana is yet to be completed. According to Gymah-Boadi, in order to achieve this, certain things, called pre-requisite for a developmental public service, should be done, namely: (1) there must be adherence to rational-legal bureaucratic principles; the public service has to be bureaucratized more not less. This means that public servants must be recruited based on merit; the public service must operate with well-defined procedures and policies, and public servants must be given appropriate incentives to put state or agency goals above personal goals; (2) key or strategic units of the public service must be insulated from political or partisan pressure; (3) administrative procedures and policies must be reformed. Therefore, administrative and political decentralization, rule simplification, and transparency must be pursued; and (4) public servants must receive adequate remuneration.[40]

The above being said, the public service cannot make change happen on its own; the state and government must work "hand-in-hand" with the Service to do this. Fortunately for Ghana, the 1992 Constitution recognized the independence of the public service through the Public Services Commission. Thus, there is some insulation from political or partisan pressure on its activities. In addition, Ghana seems to be accelerating the pace of building state capacity in the new democratic era; for instance, its creation of the value-added tax, an example of improving extractive capacity, is laudable. In the case of Ghana, the fundamentals of creating a developmental public service are being established in the new democratic era.[41]

Chapter 4

The Judiciary and its Role

Basic Structure and its Sources of Power

The Judiciary's role is to administer justice fairly to the people. This role is clearly defined in the 1992 Constitution in Articles 125, 126, and 127; its independence is emphasized. For example, Article 125, Clauses 1-5, page 91, indicates, "(1) Justice emanates from the people and shall be administered in the name of the Republic by the Judiciary which shall be independent and subject only to this Constitution. (2) Citizens may exercise popular participation in the administration of justice through the institutions of public and customary tribunals and the jury and assessor systems. (3) The judicial power of Ghana shall be vested in the Judiciary, accordingly, neither the President nor Parliament nor any organ or agency of the President or Parliament shall have or be given final judicial power. (4) The Chief Justice shall, subject to this Constitution, be the Head of the Judiciary and shall be responsible for the administration and supervision of the Judiciary. (5) The Judiciary shall have jurisdiction in all matters civil and criminal, including matters relating to this Constitution, and such other jurisdiction as Parliament may, by law, confer on it." Article 126, Clauses 1-4, pages 91-92, also states, "(1) The Judiciary shall consist of: (a) the Superior Courts of Judicature comprising: (i) the Supreme Court; (ii) the Court of Appeal; (iii) the High Court and Regional Tribunals. (b) such lower courts or tribunals as Parliament may by law establish. (2) The Superior Courts shall be superior courts of record and shall have the power to commit for contempt to themselves and all such powers as were vested in a court of record immediately before the coming into force of this Constitution. (3) Except otherwise provided in this Constitution or as may otherwise be ordered by a court in the interest of public morality, public safety or public order, the proceedings of

30

every court shall be held in public. (4) In the exercise of the judicial power conferred on the Judiciary by this Constitution or any other law, the Superior Courts may, in relation to any matter within their jurisdiction, issue such orders and directions as may be necessary to ensure the enforcement of any judgment, decree or order of those courts." Moreover, Article 127, Clauses 1-2, page 92, indicates, "(1) In the exercise of the judicial power of Ghana, the Judiciary, in both its judicial and administrative functions, including financial administration, is subject only to this Constitution and shall not be subject to the control or direction of any person or authority. (2) Neither the President nor Parliament nor any person acting under the authority of the president or Parliament nor any other persons whatsoever shall interfere with Judges or judicial officers or other persons exercising judicial power, in the exercise of their judicial functions; and all organs and agencies of the State shall accord to the courts such assistance as the courts may reasonably require to protect the independence, dignity and effectiveness of the courts, subject to this Constitution."[42]

In Articles 128-142, the functioning of the various courts is specified. Starting with Supreme Court, for instance, Article 128, Clauses 1 and 2, page 93, reiterates, "(1) The Supreme Court shall consist of the Chief Justice and not less than nine other Justices of the Supreme Court; (2) The Supreme Court shall be duly constituted for its work by not less than five Supreme Court justices." Article 129, Clauses 1 and 2, page 93-94, states, "(1) The Supreme Court shall be the final court of appeal and shall have appellate and other jurisdiction as may be conferred on it by this Constitution or by any other law. (2) The Supreme Court shall not be bound to follow the decisions of any other court." Article 136, Clauses 1 and 2, page 97, intimates "(1) The Court of Appeal shall consist of: (a) the Chief Justice; (b) subject to Clauses (2) and (3) of this Article, not less than ten justices of the Court of Appeal; and (c) such other justices of the Superior Court of Judicature as the Chief Justice may, for the determination of a particular cause or matter by writing signed by him, request to sit in the Court of Appeal for any specified period. (2) The Court of Appeal shall be duly constituted by any three of the Justices referred to in Clause (1) of this Article and when so constituted, the most senior of the justices shall preside." Additionally, Article 139, Clauses 1 and 2, pages 98-99, provides "(1) The High Court shall consist of: (a) the Chief Justice; (b) not less than twenty Justices of the High Court; and (c) such other justices of the Superior Court of Judicature as the Chief Justice may, by writing signed by him, request to sit as High Court Justices for any period. (2) The High Court shall be constituted: (a) by a single Justice of the Court; or (b) by a single Justice of the Court and jury; or (c) by a single Justice of the Court with assessors; or by three Justices of the Court for the trial of the offense of high treason. "Article 142, Clauses 1- 3, page 100, states, "(1) There shall be established in each region of Ghana such regional Tribunals as the Chief Justice may determine. (2) A Regional Tribunal shall consist of: (a) the Chief Justice; (b) one Chairman; and (c) such members who may or may not be lawyers as shall be designated by the Chief Justice to sit as panel members of a Regional Tribunal and for such period as shall be specified in writing by the Chief Justice. (3) A Regional Tribunal shall be duly constituted by a panel consisting of the Chairman and not less than two other panel members."[43] Though the 1992 Constitution allowed for Regional Tribunals, the amendment of the Courts Act of 2002, Act 620, abolished the Community and Circuit Tribunals, and established the District Courts and Circuit Courts as lower courts of the country; of course, the High Court, the Court of Appeal, and the Supreme Court are superior courts, resulting, then, in a three-tiered appeals process.[44]

The Constitution also states in Article 153, pages107-108, that "there shall be a Judicial Council, which shall comprise of the following persons: (a) the Chief Justice who will be Chairman; (b) the Attorney General; (c) a Justice of the Supreme Court nominated by the Justices of the Supreme Court; (d) a Justice of the Court of Appeal nominated by the Justices of the Court of Appeal; (e) a Justice of the High Court nominated by the Justices of the High Court; (f) two representatives of the Ghana Bar Association one of whom shall be a person of not less than twelve years' standing as a lawyer; (g) a representative of the Chairmen of Regional Tribunals nominated by the Chairmen; (h) a representative of the lower courts or tribunals; (i) the Judge Advocate-General of the Ghana Armed Forces; (j) the Head of the Legal Directorate of the Police Service; (k) the Editor of the Ghana Law Reports; (l) a representative of the Judicial Service Staff Association nominated by the Association; (m) a chief nominated by the National House of Chiefs; (n) four other persons who are not lawyers nominated by the President." The functions of the Judicial Council are clearly stated in Article 154, page 108 as: "(a) to propose for the consideration of Government, judicial reforms to improve the level of administration of justice and efficiency in the Judiciary; (b) to be a forum for consideration and discussion of matters relating to the discharge of the functions of the Judiciary and thereby assist the Chief Justice in the performance of his duties with a view to ensuring efficiency and effective realization of justice; and (c) to perform any other functions conferred on it by or under this Constitution or any other law not inconsistent with this Constitution. (2) The Judicial Council may establish such committees as it considers necessary to which it shall refer matters relating to the Judiciary."[45] Their broad role is to assist in making discharge of judicial function malleable.

Moreover, the Judicial Service, the administrative wing of the Judiciary, and part of the Public Services, is responsible for the day-to-day administration of the courts. This entity is headed by the Judicial Secretary and Deputy Judicial Secretary. There are several divisions or departments; these are Administration and Human Resources Development; Finance; Internal Audit; Information, Communication and Technology; Judicial Reforms and Projects; Communications; Works; Estate; Judicial Training Institute; Engineering and Maintenance; Facilities; Monitoring and Evaluation; Registrar General; Procurement; Logistics; Statistics; Transport; Registrar, Supreme Court; Registrar, Court of Appeal (Criminal Division); Registrar, Court of Appeal (Civil Division); Registrar, High Court; Administrator, Commercial Court; and Registrar, Land and Financial Court.[46]

Other Issues Associated with the Judiciary

According to the Africa Governance Monitoring and Advocacy Project, the Open Society Initiative for West Africa, and the Institute for Democratic Governance, the Judicial Service has made some noteworthy innovations since its inception. Two of such innovations are the establishment of the fast-track courts and the Commercial Court. The fast-track courts were established to expedite certain cases for litigants, especially those related to serious fraud.[47] The Commercial Division of the High Court (the official name of the Commercial Court), hears cases of a commercial nature, including but not limited to, banking and finance issues, the restructuring of commercial debt, and intellectual property. In this court, cases are meticulously managed by judges and strict deadlines govern trials. Adjournments are rare and are only granted for good cause. In addition, there are mandatory pre-trial conferences to be conducted within thirty days of written arguments. Mediation is also an option. Mediations are conducted by trained judges and when they fail, cases go to trial. This process has been quite successful in keeping caseloads low.[48]

Judicial effectiveness has been a key goal of administration of justice in Ghana. Therefore, in order to promote effective judicial training for judges, magistrates, and judicial staff, the Judicial Training Institute (JTI) was established in 2004. However, the genesis of this Institute did not start in 2004. In fact, previously, judges did not receive any training on appointment to the Bench from the Bar. It took the Judicial Service Act of 1960 (and Judicial Service Regulations) to establish a training school for registrars and other judicial staff in 1965. The training school, known then as the Judicial Service Training School (JSTS), did not focus on training of judges. Training of judges was mainly based on ad hoc seminars and mentoring of junior and newly-appointed judges by senior judges. However, in the mid-1970s training was extended to magistrates, and in the mid-1980s, to judges. In 1995, the JSTS was renamed the Institute of Continuing Judicial Education of Ghana (ICJEG) to take into consideration its new mandate of providing continuing education for judges and magistrates. In 2004, the ICJEG was renamed Judicial Training Institute (JTI), with the main objective of using education and training for developing the human resource needs, for judicial reform, and ensuring judicial efficiency. The JTI, therefore, develops it programs to meet the needs of the Judiciary and staff of the Judicial Service; thus, playing a key capacity-building role in the administration of justice.[49]

Ocran argues that the building of a firm and just adjudicatory system must be a major concern of the Judiciary. He emphasizes, first, that the Judiciary must subject itself to transparency and public accountability, including accountability to the representatives to the people for the use of public funds. Second, that judges must strive at balancing the public interest and the rights of the individual. Third,

35

that the Judiciary must insist on its constitutional guarantee of independence from the executive and the legislature, in order to effectively carry out its function of impartial adjudication, and also, garner the confidence of the people in the administration of justice. He states that the basic tenets of judicial independence include the following: "(1) the clear and unequivocal rejection of interference from the executive or the legislature in carrying out its adjudicatory role. This does not eschew the sort of cooperation necessary for sustaining constitutionalism or for ensuring the success of the democratic experiment; (2) enjoying institutional independence, i.e., avoidance by the legislature and the executive of the use of the power of the purse to exert undue pressure on the judiciary; (3) making decisions free from bias in the sense of favoritism for one party, inducements and improper influences, freedom from threats and pressures, and the rejection, as far as is humanly possible, of their acquired professional and class bias; and (4) the insistence on judicial adherence to very high standards of personal and professional integrity, embodied in self-regulatory codes of ethics and public law."[50]

Chapter 5

The Dynamics of Policy Making

The Policy Process

Public policy is "a set of actions by the government that includes, but not limited to, making laws and is defined in terms of a common goal or purpose."[51] For instance, a policy to make health care more affordable may include a single payer system managed solely by the government or a mixed payer system managed by the government and private insurers or government backed entities with subsidies attached for selected persons in the population. How policy comes into being or the processes leading to the policy itself is termed policy making. The power to make laws in Ghana is given to the Parliament. The laws drive the policy. The 1992 Constitution, Article 106, Clause 1, page 80, states, "The power of Parliament to make laws shall be exercised by bills passed by Parliament and assented to by the President"[52] However, for a bill to get to this stage there must be an issue, and the issue must get on the Parliamentary agenda. Once it gets onto the agenda, there is the likelihood of policy formulation. Again, the 1992 Constitution, Article 106, Clause 2, page 80, further states, "No bill, shall be introduced in Parliament unless: (a) it is accompanied by an explanatory memorandum setting out in detail the policy and principles of the bill, the defects of the existing law, the remedies proposed to deal with those defects and the necessity for its introduction; and (b) it has been published in the Gazette at least fourteen days before the date of its introduction in Parliament."[53]

Beyond this point, the subsequent steps are spelt out in Clauses 4, 5, and 7 of Article 106, page 81; and the issue on the bill becoming law is clear in Clause 11, page 82. These are specified as: "Whenever a bill is read the first time in Parliament, it shall be referred to the appropriate committee, which shall examine the bill in detail and make all such inquiries in relation to it as the committee considers expedient or necessary (Clause 4); Where a bill has been deliberated upon by the appropriate committee, it shall be reported to Parliament (Clause 5); The report of the committee, together with the explanatory memorandum to the bill, shall form the basis for a full debate on the bill for its passage, with or without amendments, or its rejection by Parliament (Clause 6); Where a bill passed by Parliament is presented to the President for assent he shall signify, within seven days after the presentation, to the Speaker that he assents to the bill or that he refuses to assent to the bill, unless the bill has been referred by the President to the Council of State (Clause 7); and Without prejudice to the power of the Parliament to postpone the operation of a law, a bill shall not become law until it has been duly passed and assented to in accordance with the provisions of this Constitution and shall not become into force unless it has been published in the Gazette (Clause 11)."[54]

From the issue coming to light, making it to the agenda of Parliament, and being referred to a committee several things happen, including roles played by key actors. There are several key actors in the policy making process, and they include higher executives; the Parliament; the Civil Service; the judiciary; other state entities such as state commissions (for example, National Development Planning Commission) and District Assemblies; the media; civil society organizations (CSOs); non-governmental organizations (NGOs) (local, regional, and international); and donors. These actors are able to make things happen or influence the policy making process. Three cases or examples of policy making processes in Ghana in recent years will be examined, including the processes involved, roles played by various actors, and the environmental conditions. The cases or examples are the Heavily Indebted Poor Country (HIPC) Watch, the Ghana National Health

Insurance Scheme (NHIS), and Environmental Policy in the Ghana Poverty Reduction Strategy Paper (PRSP). The three cases show that the policy making process is usually dominated by powerful forces and interests. Those less powerful in society are generally marginalized, probably, not intentionally, but by the very process itself.

The first case or example is HIPC Watch. In this case or example Kamara and Yeboah,[55] describe how the Social Enterprise Development Foundation of West Africa popularly called SEND, recognizing the challenge of how to engage pro-poor and grassroots-based CSOs in the Ghana Poverty Reduction Strategy (GPRS) decided to do something about it. The GPRS was linked to or based on Ghana joining the HIPC Debt Relief Initiative. SEND focused on building the capacity of civil society groups and local government officials in resource-poor Northern Ghana. This project had three objectives: build awareness of CSOs on the GPRS; establish and strengthen the monitoring capacity of CSOs so that they can collaborate with SEND to carry out participatory monitoring and evaluation of the HIPC Debt Relief Initiative on the poor in twenty-five districts in Northern Ghana; and strengthen District Assemblies (DAs) and CSOs partnership in the implementation of the GPRS. To achieve the objectives, SEND targeted district-based development NGOs, faith-based organizations, women's groups, youth groups, farmers, and persons with disabilities to partner with them to develop and implement the Ghana HIPC Watch (GHW). In all thirty CSOs participated in the process. Although the CSOs agreed to partner with SEND, they expressed reservations about the implications. The CSOs were skeptical about whether the government will accept their critique or monitoring of national policies and/or programs regarding HIPC. The reason was the majority, if not all, had not participated in such an exercise before; they had limited skills and experience dealing with the government on policy matters.

To increase understanding of and engagement in the GPRS, SEND organized workshops for the CSOs, and these workshops were supported by the Ghana National Development Planning Commission, a governmental entity charged with the responsibility for development, monitoring, and evaluation of the GPRS. One outcome of the workshops was the declaration of the need for GHW to follow-up and continue the educational process by providing guidance and training on policy advocacy. The education phase was followed by the participatory monitoring and evaluation (PME) phase. This phase entailed organizing workshops on how to gather information among other things. The CSOs which participated in these workshops were approved by the DAs. After the workshops were completed, 15 CSOs were elected to form the District HIPC Monitoring Committee (DHMC) to monitor HIPC funded programs. It was also agreed that the PME will be guided by three broad indicators: good governance, accountability, and equity as these were lacking from the central government's implementation of HIPC programs; thus, they were also seen as challenges. Regarding good governance, GHW advocacy activities emphasized promoting participation of DAs in decision-making at the national level. The involvement of project beneficiaries in project identification and implementation were identified as an important issue at the district level. Taking into consideration accountability, the emphasis was on making HIPC financial accounts district-based in order to reduce transaction costs and make them easily accessible to administrators, contractors, and project beneficiaries. In relation to equity, the channeling of resources equally to groups was critical; for instance, addressing the needs of women in a holistic manner was a common theme. Microcredit provision, reproductive rights and education (especially for young girls) were key recommendations for equity. Through HIPC Watch, grassroots CSOs can engage in policy monitoring and evaluation to enhance the impact of policies on the poor in society. As a result of capacity building for CSOs and district level government officials, a very strong partnership has developed. It has improved information gathering and sharing; increased citizens' interest in governance at the district level; and increased calls for extension of monitoring to other sectors of the economy such as the DAs and the parliamentary common fund. The local CSOs now have the attention of the DAs, Parliament, and some governmental agencies. The key actors were: the regional NGO, SEND; grassroots development-based CSOs; DAs; and National Development Planning Commission. These worked together in policy advocacy to build awareness of CSOs on GPRS; build capacity of CSOs and DAs to monitor and evaluate HIPC projects; strengthen DAs and partnership between SEND on the one hand, and the DAs and CSOs on the other. The environment was ripe for the CSOs participating in and monitoring HIPC projects, and SEND took advantage of this environment to create awareness and involvement of the participants in the HIPC projects. It is a case of an NGO helping CSOs to participate in the policy process.

The second case or example is the NHIS. In this case or example, Agyepong and Adjei[56] discuss the processes that took place during the development, enactment, and implementation of the NHIS. The authors elucidate on how key actors, especially policy elite, the environment, the agenda-setting circumstances, and policy characteristics interplayed to bring about a policy shift in Ghana's health care system. The health care system was unpopular with the population due to the out-of-pocket fees at point of service called cash-and-carry, and the New Patriotic Party (NPP) promised during the campaign of 2000 that it will change that system if elected to power.

The NPP won that election and took over power in January 2001, and subsequently in March 2001, the Minister of Health appointed a seven-member task force, with the Director for Policy Planning, Monitoring and Evaluation in the said Ministry as its chairman. The members were either technocrats or were critical stakeholders from the Ministry of Health, Ghana Health Service, Dangme West District Directorate and Research Center, Trades Union Congress, and Ghana Health Care Company. The Task Force was given a charge based on 4 tenets: (1) to support and advice the Minister of Health on the development of a NHIS; (2) the building up of systems and capacity for regulation of health insurance in Ghana; (3) the development of appropriate health insurance legislation; and (4) the mobilization of extra resources to support national health insurance. As deliberations went on, the Minister expressed that he wanted a centralized single payer scheme. However, the chair and other members of the task force disagreed with that idea. Conflict ensued between the Minister and the chair, and the chair then chose to cease participation in deliberations. Consequently, the work of the task force slowed down greatly. As a result of these developments, the Minister removed the chair, brought in a trusted associate to be chair, and gradually the new chair also brought in trusted associates, referred to as political elites (i.e., those well-connected politically who help shape policy) to be members of the task force. In the end, a hybrid which had a single payer scheme for the formal sector and multiple payer types for the informal sector emerged, which the Minister was satisfied with. However, not long after, there was a cabinet reshuffle and the Minister of Health was reassigned to another Ministry.

The new Minister of Health continued the process of fine tuning the output of the task force, but with time, the political associates dominated the deliberations, and the suggestions or ideas of the technocratic members were ignored. So, one by one the technocrats either resigned or quietly left the task force. By the time of making the final decision on the NHIS in 2002, only one of the original members was left. In January 2003, the final version of the National Health Insurance bill was introduced in Parliament, one week before recess, under an urgency certificate to be fast tracked into law. A one-week window was given for the bill to be debated and passed into law. In the mean time, not many had seen the final version of the bill before it was introduced. The preceding events caused organized labor groups such as the Civil Servants Association, Ghana National Association of Teachers, Ghana Registered Nurses Association, Judicial Services Workers Union, and Trade Union Congress as well as the main opposition party, National Democratic Congress (NDC) to protest the bill. In response, the bill was withdrawn temporarily. In August 2003, Parliament was called back from recess, and the bill was re-introduced to be debated and voted on; the opposition expressed concerns and reservations about rushing the bill through Parliament. Nonetheless, the ruling party went on and passed the bill anyway, because it had the numbers to do so. This then became the National Health Insurance Act of 2003, Act 650. This Act resulted in establishing the NHIS governed by the National Health Insurance Council. The Act allowed the formal and informal sector to enroll together in government sponsored district Mutual Health Organizations (MHOs). Although it allowed private MHOs, the government would not give any funds to such MHOs. It also spelt out how the NHIS will be funded.

After passage of the bill, technical committees were formed to implement the Law. The committees included technocrats and political associates (the same ones on the task force). The chairman of the task force became the chairman of the Implementation Steering Committee. Contrary to expectations of the technocrats, in this instance also, the political elites dominated the process and deliberations. In fact, many of them were consultants to the setting up of the MHOs in the districts. When the NPP came back to power in January 2005, and in the wake of protests against activities of the political elites and/or consultants, the new Minister of Health ordered an audit of the NHIS. This development resulted in the dismissal of the first chief executive officer, the political consultants were dropped, and a new chief executive officer for the NHIS was hired. Subsequently, a more technical, or more appropriately a balanced, approach was pursued. The key actors were: the Ministers of Health; appointed chairs; political elites or consultants; labor groups; NPP members of parliament; NDC members of parliament; private MHOs; and donors. This is a case where political elites took over a policy process. Politics was paramount to technical issues in development and formulation of policy. Later on, in the implementation phase, technical issues became more paramount to political issues. An analysis shows, there was support for health reform (issue) in the general population (environment), a promise to create change in health policy by a political party which later became the government (agenda-setting), and the issue was debated in the public arena (policy characteristic). The issue was later developed into a law and policy. This case shows that flexibility is essential in policy making. It adds credence to the notion that it is sound practice, in the long-term, not to tilt too much to either the political or technical side of an issue or policy. The stakeholder or policy maker should know when to be political and when to be technical.

The third case or example is Environmental Policy in the Ghana Poverty Reduction Strategy Paper. In this case or example, the Knowledge, Technology and Society Team of the Institute of Development Studies at the University of Sussex[57] use discourse/narratives (what is the policy narrative? How is it framed through science, research, etc?); actors/networks (who is involved and how are they

44

connected?); politics/interests (what are the underlying power dynamics?); and policy spaces (the extent to which policy makers are restricted in decision-making by forces such as opinions of dominant actors/networks) to explain how land and environmental policy was hijacked by powerful political and elite interests.

The traditional narratives regarding land and the environment in the Ghana Poverty Reduction Strategy (GPRS) emphasize technical modernization, economic growth, and the need for environmental audit and technical impact assessments. That is, the focus is on equity, the need to reform the land tenure system, and market-led policies; such a view is considered apolitical. The alternative narratives, however, emphasize the power of extractive industries, importance of multiple uses of land to rural residents, need for debate on trade-offs, control and access, and on residents' rights to land as opposed to a conduit for equity. These latter views deal with politics of access and control as well as regulation. They fundamentally question the apolitical perspective of the GPRS. In the environmental policy arena, there are two networks; the first is made up of policy makers in various government departments and donors, who tend to believe in traditional narratives. In this group are powerful vested interests such as well-connected politicians, business people, the mining lobby (specifically, the Chamber of Mines), and some government officials. The second is made up of environmental organizations (NGOs), traditional leaders, and journalists, who tend to believe in the alternative narratives. The emphasis on the traditional narratives that push for technological development and economic growth favored the powerful interests in the gold mining and timber industries. At the time of the reform, it appeared as if the government was "in bed" with these interests for some political loyalty or benefits. Either way, donors who supported the poverty reduction strategy were more focused on the technical rather than the political.

45

In fact, developing the GPRS was a participatory process involving several groups or so it appeared. The groups included; government ministers, religious leaders, NGOs, village residents, the media, women's groups, and trade unions. However, participation or involvement varied from minimal (informed with no input) to heavily involved (full-scale participation) depending on one's status politically and/or socially. Even in the latter case, ministers with access to funding, access to international consultancies, and technical expertise had more sway. This resulted in the core issues of poverty's relatedness to environmental degradation, inequality, and development to be minimally dealt with in the initiatives, and hence, the outcome was more technical than otherwise (i.e., emphasis on traditional narratives). A way forward or to deal with this shortcoming is to revisit the document or strategy, and address participation and concerns of local residents and civil society and/or environmental groups. This review and action will result in focusing more on the alternative narratives, such as environmental rights to resource, or at least, striking a balance between the two narratives. The key actors were the Ministry of Lands and Natural Resources officials, Chamber of Mines, political elites, business elites, NGOs, traditional leaders, media, and residents. This is a case where government actors and powerful interests, and to a lesser extent donors, used policy narratives, networks, politics/interests as well as policy space to craft land and environmental policy in the GPRS that focused more on technical rather than on social, political, and economic factors, or at least, including them in the Strategy. The question of, "who has rights to or control over land", were ignored. In the end, powerful interests won; the less powerful had to "make do."

The Parliamentary Service

The day-to-day administration of Parliament is carried out by the Parliamentary Service, which is part of the Public services. The Parliamentary

Service was established by the Parliamentary Service Act of 1993, Act 640. It derives its power from the 1992 Constitution, Article 124, Clauses 1-5, pages 89 and 90. These clauses state: "(1) There shall be a Parliamentary Service which shall form part of the public services of Ghana. (2) There shall be a Parliamentary Service Board which shall consist of: (a) the Speaker as Chairman; (b) four other members all of whom shall be appointed by the Speaker acting in accordance with the advice of a committee of Parliament; and (c) the Clerk to the Parliament. (3) There shall be a Clerk to Parliament who shall be the head of the Parliamentary Service. (4) The appointment of the Clerk and the other members of his staff in the Parliamentary Service shall be made by the Parliamentary Service Board in consultation with the Public Services Commission. (5) The Parliamentary Service Board shall, with the prior approval of Parliament, make regulations, by constitutional instrument, prescribing the terms and conditions of service of the officers and other employees in the Parliamentary Service and generally for the effective and efficient administration of the Parliamentary Service."[58]

As indicated in the Constitution, therefore, the Parliamentary Service has a governing board, the Parliamentary Service Board, of six members comprising the Speaker as chair, the Clerk to the Parliament, and four others. The Clerk as head of the Parliamentary Service is assisted by three deputies, heads of departments, and other specialized officers. The key functions of the Parliamentary Service are to: "(1) facilitate the work of Parliament through the provision of support services to the House, including its committees and agencies for the purpose of ensuring full and effective exercise of the powers of the Parliament, and (2) enhance the dignity of the House and adequately inform the public on Parliamentary activities." A corollary to these functions is to demonstrate transparency, impartiality, and a high-sense of professionalism. In short, the Parliamentary Service makes the Parliament run smoothly.[59]

Chapter 6

Conclusion: Tying All Together

Public administration occurs mostly in the executive branch, usually through the Civil Service and other governmental entities. These entities comprise the Ministries, departments, public boards, commissions, corporations, and services. Examples of such entities are the Ministry of Finance, Ministry of Food and Agriculture, Ministry of Transport, Ministry of Health, Ministry of Information and Media Relations, Ministry of Justice and Attorney General's Department, Office of the Head of Civil Service, Social Security and National Insurance Trust, Bank of Ghana, Controller and Accountant General's Department, Ghana Standards Authority, Food and Drugs Authority, Ghana Ports and Harbors Authority, and Lands Commission. Furthermore, there are specialized independent public commissions, such as the Commission on Human Rights and Administrative Justice (CHRAJ) and the National Commission for Civic Education (NCCE). All these entities derive their authority from the Constitution, Acts of Parliament, and other laws. Moreover, these entities are conduits through which the government carries out laws of the nation or its programs to the citizens. The Civil Service is a key hub in carrying out governmental programs, and it has its roots in the colonial days of British rule. However, the current Civil Service is governed by PNDCL 327 of 1993, which makes the Civil Service part of the Public Services. Over the years, the Civil Service has undergone reforms as a result of poor performance and/or effectiveness. Some of the reforms are the Civil Service Reform Program (CSRP), Civil Service Performance Improvement Program (CSPIP), and New Approach to Public Sector Reform (NAPSR). Results of these reforms are mixed; yet, there is hope because movement is in the positive direction to create a developmental public service. The Judiciary also plays a critical role in administering justice. It is

49

governed by the Judicial Council and its day-to-day administration is under the purview of the Judicial Service. However, the overall authority of the Judiciary lies with the Chief Justice. The Judiciary has put pillars in place to be a professional effective and independent arm of the government.

Policy making in Ghana, as expected, is dynamic and includes issue identification, agenda-setting, policy formulation, policy implementation, and monitoring and evaluation. In Ghana, as in most countries, policy formulation and enactment is primarily the purview of Parliament, the legislature. However, policy is not made in a vacuum; the policy process involves several stakeholders, especially key actors. These key actors are the ones who can make or break policy, because of their unique influence on the policy process. Three cases or examples of the policy process in action are the Heavily Indebted Poor Country (HIPC) Watch, the Ghana National Health Insurance Scheme (NHIS), and Environmental Policy in the Ghana Poverty Reduction Strategy Paper (PRSP). What's more, Parliament does not function in a vacuum. It is assisted in its day-to-day operation by the Parliamentary Service, which is given overall policy direction by the Parliamentary Service Board. It is the object of the Service to be transparent and impartial in the discharge of its duties.

It is necessary to have and/or develop appropriate institutional frameworks or structures for effective administration to take place. The fruits of effective administration and policy making will obviously transfer to the citizens and, consequently, lead to a measure of satisfaction. Effective public administration and policy making is not error-free, however, constant refining will result in improved performance of public institutions and those who influence administration and policy. Ghana is attempting to improve its public administration delivery and policy making process, striving step-by-step, to build the appropriate frameworks to effect administration and policy making in an efficient manner.

Endnotes

*Listed objectives as well as functions of boards, commissions, and other governmental entities are provided from those organizations.

References

1. Milakovich, M.E., and G.J. Gordon. (2009). Public Administration in America, 10th ed. Boston, MA: Wadsworth Cengage Learning.

2. Constitution. (1992). Republic of Ghana Constitution. Tema, Ghana: Ghana Publishing Corporation.

3. Government of Ghana. (2013). "Ministries." http://www.ghana.gov.gh [Retrieved May 28, 2013].

4. Adum-Yeboah, P. (2011). 2012 Budget Highlights: Commentary. Accra, Ghana: PricewaterhouseCoopers (Ghana) Limited.

5. Ministry of Finance. (2013). "Departments." http://www.mofep.gov.gh [Retrieved May 28, 2013].

6. Ministry of Food and Agriculture. (2013). "About the Ministry of Food and Agriculture." http://www.mofa.gov.gh [Retrieved July 23, 2013].

7. Ministry of Transport. (2013). "Departments and Agencies." http://www.mot.gov.gh [Retrieved May 28, 2013].

8. Ministry of Health. (2013). "Directorates." http://www.moh-ghana.org [Retrieved May 28, 2013].

9. Government of Ghana. (2013). "Ministry of Information." http://www.ghana.gov.gh [Retrieved May 28, 2013].

10. Government of Ghana. (2013). "Ministry of Justice and Attorney General's Department." http://www.ghana.gov.gh [Retrieved May 28, 2013].

11. Constitution. (1992). Republic of Ghana Constitution. Tema, Ghana: Ghana Publishing Corporation.

12. Public Services Commission. (2013). "About Us." http://www.psc.gov.gh [Retrieved April 24, 2013].

13. Kiggundu, M.N. (1996). "A Longitudinal Study of the Size, Cost and Administrative Reform of the African Civil Service." Journal of African Finance and Economic Development 2 (1): 77-107.

14. Agyekum-Dwamena, N.A. (2003). "Ghana Civil Service in Context: A Constraint or an Opportunity for Improving Performance in Public Organizations?" http://www.public.iastate.edu/~fowusu/AccraWorkshop/Wkshp_Appendix_C.pdf [Retrieved July 3, 2013].

15. OHCS. (2013). "Various Headings." http://www.ohcs.gov.gh/ [Retrieved May 28, 2013].

16. Ibid.

17. SSNIT. (2013). "Various Headings." http://www.ssnit.org.gh/ [Retrieved May 28, 2013].

18. Bank of Ghana. (2013). "Various Headings." http://www.bog.gov.gh/ [Retrieved May 28, 2013].

19. Controller and Accountant General's Department. (2013). "Various Headings." http://cagd.gov.gh/ [Retrieved June 2, 2013].

20. Ghana Standards Authority. (2013). "Various Headings." http://www.gsa.gov.gh/ [Retrieved May 29, 2013].

21. Public Health Act. (2012). "Act 851." http://www.tobaccocontrollaws.org/files/live/Ghana/Ghana-Pub.Health.Act2012-national.pdf [Retrieved May 15, 2013]; Food and Drugs Authority. (2013). "Various Headings." http://www.fdbghana.gov.gh/ [Retrieved May 29, 2013].

22. Ghana Ports and Harbors Authority. (2013). "About Us." http://www.ghanaports.gov.gh [Retrieved June 3, 2013].

23. Lands Commission. (2010). "New Lands Commission in Place." http://www.ghanalap.gov.gh/index1.php?Linkedid=281 [Retrieved June 2, 2013].

24. CHRAJ. (2014). "Various Headings." http://www.chrajghana.com/ [Retrieved January 17, 2014].

25. Ibid.

26. NCCE. (2014). "Various Headings." http://nccegh.org/ [Retrieved January 18, 2014].

27. The Presidency of the Republic of Ghana. (2013). "Office of the Head of Civil Service." http://www.presidency.gov.gh/our-government/agencies-commissions/office-head-civil-service [Retrieved July 3, 2013].

28. Ibid.

29. Ibid.

30. Agyekum-Dwamena, N.A. (2003). "Ghana Civil Service in Context: A Constraint or an Opportunity for Improving Performance in Public Organizations?" http://www.public.iastate.edu/~fowusu/AccraWorkshop/Wkshp_Appendix_C.pdf [Retrieved July 3, 2013].

31. Adei, A., and Y. Boachie-Danquah. (2002). "The Civil Service Performance Improvement Program (CSPIP) in Ghana: Lessons of Experience." Paper Presented at the 24th AAPAM Annual Roundtable Conference on the African Public Service in the 21st Century-New Initiatives in Performance Management, November 25-19, Lesotho Sun Hotel, Maseru, Lesotho.

32. Agyekum-Dwamena, N.A. (2003). "Ghana Civil Service in Context: A Constraint or an Opportunity for Improving Performance in Public Organizations?" http://www.public.iastate.edu/~fowusu/AccraWorkshop/Wkshp_Appendix_C.pdf [Retrieved July 3, 2013].

33. Kiggundu, M.N. (1996). "A Longitudinal Study of the Size, Cost and Administrative Reform of the African Civil Service." Journal of African Finance and Economic Development 2 (1):77-107.

34. Ayee, J.R.A. (2001). "Civil Service Reform in Ghana: A Case Study of Contemporary Reform Problems in Africa." African Journal of Political Science 6 (1): 1-41.

35. Ibid.

36. Ibid.

37. Adei, A., and Y. Boachie-Danquah. (2002). "The Civil Service Performance Improvement Program (CSPIP) in Ghana: Lessons of Experience." Paper Presented at the 24th AAPAM Annual Roundtable Conference on the African Public Service in the 21st Century-New Initiatives in Performance Management, November 25-19, Lesotho Sun Hotel, Maseru, Lesotho.

38. Agyekum-Dwamena, N.A. (2003). "Ghana Civil Service in Context: A Constraint or an Opportunity for Improving Performance in Public Organizations?" http://www.public.iastate.edu/~fowusu/AccraWorkshop/Wkshp_Appendix_C.pdf [Retrieved July 3, 2013].

39. Holm-Graves, G. (2011). "The New Approach to Public Sector Reform." http://www.ghana.gov.gh/index.php/news/features/4691-the-new-approach-to-public-sector-reform [Retrieved July 7, 2013].

40. Gyimah-Boadi, E. (2004). The Search for a Developmental Public Service in Ghana: Challenges and Prospects. Paper Presented at the 7th Annual Lecture of the Public Services Commission, May 19, Teachers Hall, Accra, Ghana.

41. Ibid.

42. Constitution. (1992). Republic of Ghana Constitution. Tema, Ghana: Ghana Publishing Corporation.

43. Ibid.

44. Judicial Service. (2013). "Various Headings." http://www.judicial.gov.gh/ [Retrieved January 15, 2014].

45. Constitution. (1992). Republic of Ghana Constitution. Tema, Ghana: Ghana Publishing Corporation.

46. Judicial Service. (2013). "Various Headings." http://www.judicial.gov.gh/ [Retrieved January 15, 2014].

47. Africa Governance Monitoring and Advocacy Project, Open Society Initiative for West Africa, and Institute for Democratic Governance. (2007). Ghana Justice Sector and the Rule of Law: A Discussion Paper. Open Society Initiative for West Africa, Dakar, Senegal.

48. Cofie, S. (2007). "Ghana-Establishment of the Commercial Court." SmartLessons, December, International Finance Corporation, World Bank Group, Washington, DC.

49. Judicial Service. (2013). "Various Headings." http://www.judicial.gov.gh/ [Retrieved January 15, 2014].

50. Ocran, M. (2008). "Nation Building in Africa and the Role of the Judiciary." Northern Illinois University Law Review 28: 169-182.

51. Cochran, C.E., L.C. Mayer, T.R. Carr, N.J. Cayer, M.J. McKenzie, and L.R. Peck. (2012). American Public Policy: An Introduction, 10th ed. Boston, MA: Wadsworth Cengage Learning.

52. Constitution. (1992). Republic of Ghana Constitution. Tema, Ghana: Ghana Publishing Corporation.

53. Ibid.

54. Ibid.

55. Kamara, S., and H. Yeboah. (2005). Bringing the Poor into Advocacy: A Look at Ghana HIPC Watch. Social Enterprise Development Foundation of West Africa, Accra, Ghana.

56. Agyepong, I.A., and S. Adjei. (2008). "Public Social Policy Development and Implementation: A Case Study of the Ghana Health Insurance Scheme." Health Policy and Planning 23: 150-160.

57. Knowledge, Technology and Society Team. (2006). Understanding Policy Processes: A Review of IDS Research on the Environment. Institute of Development Studies, University of Sussex, Brighton, UK.

58. Constitution. (1992). Republic of Ghana Constitution. Tema, Ghana: Ghana Publishing Corporation.

59.   Parliamentary   Service.   (2014).   "Various   Headings." http://www.parliament.gh/content/389/41[Retrieved January 16, 2014].

APPENDIX

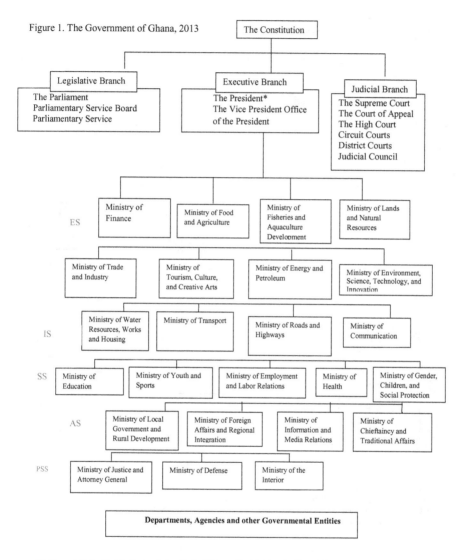

Figure 1. The Government of Ghana, 2013

ES= Economic Sector; IS= Infrastructure Sector; SS= Social Sector; AS= Administration Sector; PSS= Public Safety Sector

Source: Figure Developed by Author; Sector Divisions: Adopted from Adum-Yeboah, P. (2011). 2012 Budget Highlights: Commentary.
*There is a Council of State that plays an advisory role to the President

Figure 2. Bank of Ghana Organizational Structure, 2013

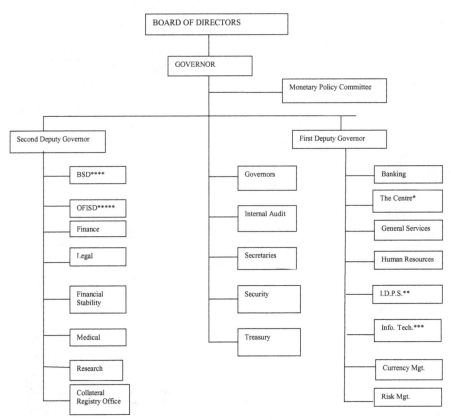

*The Centre= Centre for Training & Professional Development
**IDPS= Information, Documentation and Publication Services
***Info. Tech = Information Technology
****BSD = Banking Supervision Department
*****OFISD= Other Financial Institutions Supervision Department

Source: Bank of Ghana (2013) http://www.bog.gov.gh/privatecontent//Public-
Affairs/ BANKOF GHANA.ORGANIZATIONALSTRUCTURE-2013.pdf

Figure 3. Ghana Standards Authority Organizational Chart, 2013

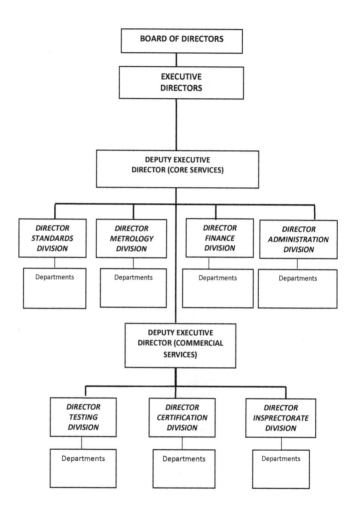

Source: Ghana Standard Authority. (2013) http://www.gsa.gov.gh/site/Chart/organizational_chart.pdf
phpMyAdmin=2dc4ecf5c1abt1.ce2db13